Beneath the Surface

Ron Benson
Lynn Bryan
Kim Newlove
Charolette Player
Liz Stenson

CONSULTANTS
Kathyrn D'Angelo
Susan Elliott-Johns
Diane Lomond
Ken MacInnis
Elizabeth Parchment

Prentice Hall Ginn Canada
Scarborough, Ontario

Contents

Selections with this symbol are available on audio.

This symbol indicates student writing.

Canadian selections are marked with this symbol.

Coral: At Home on a Reef

by K. M. DeCelles

It's a beautiful day in the neighborhood. The coral reef neighborhood, that is. Thousands of kinds of animals, including this reef shark, call the coral reef home. They depend on it for hiding, hunting, breeding, and eating. Want to meet some other neighbors? Just keep reading.

Happy to Be Stuck

Sitting on the reef, a file shell (below) "tastes" the water with its long tentacles. Then it uses them to catch tiny bits of floating food.

But sitting on the reef can be a problem for a creature that can't hang on! The waves could easily sweep it away.

So the file shell has a trick. It attaches itself to the coral with sticky threads. That way, it's stuck tight to its coral home—right where it wants to be.

Big Guys, Little Guys

Coral reefs are hard, stony shapes built by tiny animals called polyps (POL-ups). Each polyp builds a little "house" around itself. A coral reef is made of thousands of these houses built on top of each other over the years.

A reef is many things to many creatures. For a white-tip reef shark (page 4), it's a place to find fishy meals. But for the violet-spotted reef lobster (below), it's a place full of holes for hiding from enemies.

Looking for Lunch

With its glowing stripes, this little triplefin (above) is a sight to see. And you might say it's sightseeing too. The fish uses the coral as a "lookout tower," propping itself up on its fins as if they were hands. Then it watches for tiny creatures that might be good to eat.

Stick It to 'Em

Christmas trees on a coral reef? Nope, these are strange animals called Christmas-tree worms (right).

Each worm lives in a hard tube it has built on the coral. If a hungry fish comes along, the worm quickly disappears into its tube. All that's left is a hard, sharp spike. Now if that fish tries to wolf down the worm, it may get a sharp surprise!

Cruising the Neighborhood

A nudibranch (NU-duh-brank) is a fancy snail without a shell (above). It cruises the coral neighborhood, eating algae (AL-jee). Algae are tiny plants that grow on the reef.

As the nudibranch moves along, its bright colors warn enemies that it tastes bad.

Meals Are Just an Arm's Length Away

The coral reef has plenty of cozy holes for an octopus (left) to live in. It hides there until a tasty crab or other creature comes along.

When one does, watch out! A sucker-covered arm snakes out of the hole and grabs the prey. Then the octopus pulls the wriggling catch into the hole. For this coral-reef creature, dinner is served!

Long Nose for Nipping

For the long-nosed butterfly fish (right), the coral reef is like a big lunch counter! That's because this fish likes to munch on tiny coral polyps.

Lots of fish's mouths would be too big to grab hold of the little polyps. But the butterfly fish has a tiny mouth at the end of a long, pointy snout. It's the perfect tool for plucking polyps from their stony coral houses.

Sneaky Snacking

This lizard fish (below) is lying on the coral, waiting for a small fish or other creature to get close enough to catch.

Some fish may think they could take a little nip out of the big fish and dart quickly away, but the hungry lizard fish would probably dart faster!

Just Us Corals Here

The trumpet fish (right) is tricky. It hides tail-up in a kind of coral shaped like its body. When a small fish swims near, the trumpet fish goes after it.

The prey fish may see the trumpet fish coming. But that pencil-thin body looks pretty small from the front. And if the prey fish gets fooled, the trumpet fish gets fed.

A Nose Job

A ribbon eel (left) has a long, skinny body—perfect for fitting into long, skinny holes in the reef.

The eel's feathery nostrils are long too. They're great for tasting or smelling odors in the water. So the eel can tell when prey or enemies are near, without having to come out of its hole. Guess you could say its nose knows!

"Leaf" This Fish Alone

This sail-fin leaf fish (below) lies on the reef waiting. It looks like a leaf waving in the waves. But when a small fish comes close, the "leaf" leaps to life and eats it up.

Now that your visit is over, all the neighbors want you to know: a coral reef is a nice place to visit. But for them, it's a great place to live!

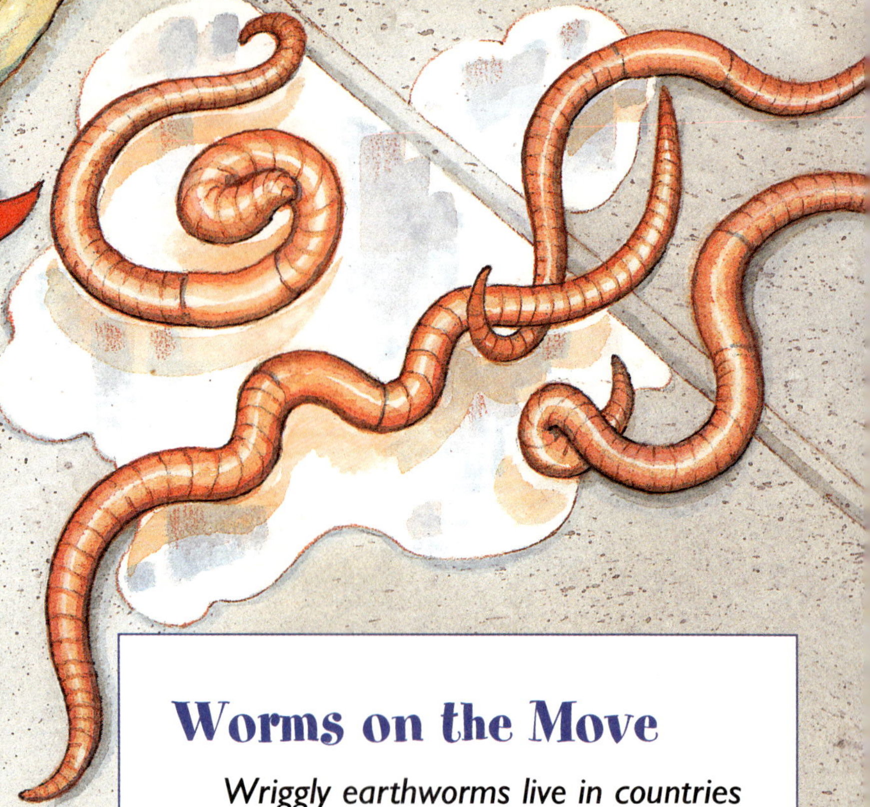

Worm Ways and Ant Antics

by Diane Swanson
Illustrated by Renée Mansfield

Worms on the Move

Wriggly earthworms live in countries all over the world. Some live in your backyard. You see them on lawns or roads on rainy days. But usually worms live underground in cool, damp soil where they stay moist. Worms breathe through their skins. If they dry out, the worms die.

Earthworms have no eyes, no ears, no nose, no teeth, no legs, and no bones. But they are some of the world's most important animals. They plow the soil, letting in air and water. As they tunnel along, they swallow soil and dead plant and animal matter. Then they create little piles of soil mixed with waste. All this helps plants grow, making food for animals and people.

Unearth an Earthworm

Tools

- Small shovel or trowel
- Newspaper

Steps

1. Go outside on a dark, cloudy day. Earthworms avoid light.
2. Walk softly. Worms sense your footsteps.
3. Dig in a damp place in a garden, or beneath a tree or rock.

4. Dump big scoops of soil on a newspaper.
5. Spread out the soil. GENTLY feel for a large worm.
6. Hold the worm and put the soil back.

Be a Worm Whiz

Tools

- Magnifying glass

Steps

1. Feel how soft and moist the earthworm is.
2. Look at the 100 to 200 muscle rings in its body.
3. Find the worm's head and tail by looking for a wide, light-colored band. It is closer to the head.
4. Find the worm's top and bottom. No matter how you place the worm, it will turn itself topside up.
5. Gently slide your finger along the bottom of the worm—from tail to head. You can feel hundreds of tiny bristles. They help the worm move. They also help it hold tight to its underground burrow if a bird tries to pull the worm out.

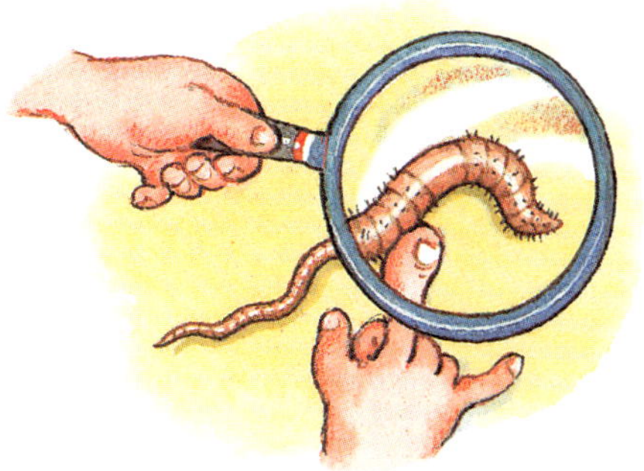

6. Use your magnifying glass to see the bristles.

Watch a Worm

Tools

- Cake pan
- 4 sheets of toilet paper, stacked and dampened

Steps

1. Put the damp toilet paper over part of the pan.
2. GENTLY place the earthworm—half on the pan, half on the paper. Watch which way it moves.

3. Do this several times. The worm will prefer the paper. It is damp and uneven—like soil. The pan is smooth and hard to grip with bristles.
4. Watch how the worm moves. It stretches its front end out like an elastic, then the tail end follows.
5. Release the worm where you found it and watch it burrow back into the soil, or under leaves or rocks.

6. Lie face down in the grass, your legs together, arms by your sides. Try to move like a worm.

Wonder Worms Around the World

- Worms can move 50 times their weight. That's like you pushing a rhinoceros.
- 50 000 worms can live in a big backyard.
- There are about 3000 kinds of earthworms.
- Longest earthworm: about 3.5 metres, almost as long as two beds placed end to end.
- Shortest earthworm: about 1 millimetre, the width of a pencil lead.

The Ants Go Marching

There are thousands of different kinds of ants on earth. But all kinds are social, which means they live and work together. That's what makes ants unlike most other insects. And that's why so many scientists want to learn more about ants.

All the ants that live in one nest come from the eggs of one ant—the queen. She looks after her first set of ants until they grow. Then they look after her and the other eggs she lays. Soon there are more and more of these worker ants. They find food for the ant colony, protect the young, clean the nest, and so on.

Analyze an Ant

Tools

- Magnifying glass

Steps

1. Watch for an ant on a warm fall day. Ants usually don't leave their nests if it's colder than 12°C.
2. Follow that ant and see what it does. When it stops, use your magnifying glass to see its big eyes and the feelers it uses to smell and touch. You may see it clean its feelers, pulling them through long leg hairs. Ants clean themselves often.
3. Check the ant's mouth—designed to chew, dig, build, carry, and fight. And try to see its claws, which help the ant climb trees.

4. Make a small puddle of water in front of an ant, blocking its way. Notice how it avoids water and walks around the puddle. Ants can drown in water.
5. Find an ant nest. Look under a rock or some firewood. If you uncover a nest, you may see many worker ants running for safety. GENTLY set the rock or firewood back the way it was. The ants will return when they sense it's safe.

Amazing Ants

- An ant can lift 50 times its own weight. That's like you lifting a rhinoceros.
- Some farming ants grow their own food—a fungus. They chew up leaves to make fertilizer for their gardens.
- Shortest worker ant: about 0.8 millimetres, less than the width of a pencil lead.
- Longest worker ant: about 33 millimetres, slightly longer than the average paper clip.

Treat an Ant

Tools

- Honey
- Bread crust
- A juicy fruit, like a pear

Steps

1. Dip a small bit of bread crust in honey and drop it in front of an ant.
2. Watch closely to see if the ant carries the food in its mouth or eats it. If the ant eats the food, it may go into the ant's second stomach, which is used to carry food back to the nest.

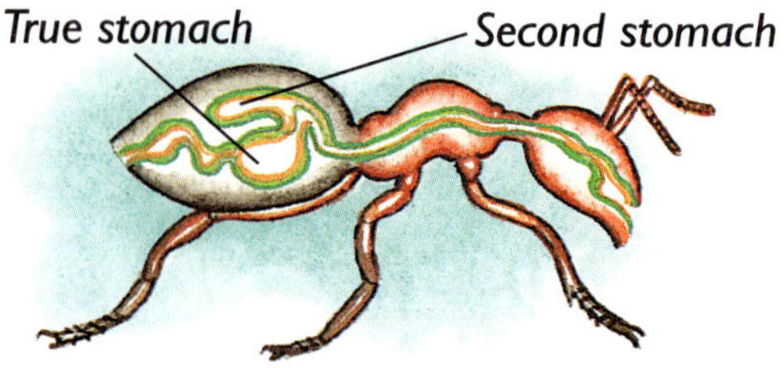

3. Place half of a juicy fruit near some ants. They may suck out some of the juice with their mouths, then go back to the nest. Because they're excited about finding the fruit, their bodies leave a trail along the way. You can't see it, but the ants in the nest can smell it. They will likely follow the trail to the fruit.

4. Watch to see if more and more ants come to the fruit. Count the number that come. See how long it takes them to suck most of the fruit.

The Big Sleep

by Tracey Randinelli

Winter is on its way. For many animals, it's going to be tough to find food and stay warm during the cold winter months. What will they do? They won't sweat it—they'll sleep through it! Lots of animals spend anywhere from a few weeks to several months in a sleep-like state called hibernation. During hibernation, an animal's temperature and heart rate drop, and its breathing slows almost to a standstill. That way, it uses much less energy than it normally needs. When the weather gets warmer, the animal wakes up rested and ready for some summer fun!

Light Sleeper

A few months of winter shut-eye isn't enough for the tiny dormouse. This little guy spends half the year hibernating! During the summer, the dormouse stores up body fat by stuffing itself with fruits and seeds. In October, it hits the sack in a "bed" of leaves and grass. During the next few months, the dormouse breathes just once every couple of minutes. Its heartbeat drops from about three hundred beats per minute to just ten or so, and its temperature falls from 37°C to as low as 4°C. When spring arrives, the dormouse wakes up ready for a snack. You can't blame him—in that half year, the dormouse can lose up to half its body weight!

Full House ▶

Garter snakes don't like to be alone during their long winter nap. The solution to this knotty problem? Hundreds—even thousands—often hibernate together in one huge, spaghetti-like clump. The body heat of all those snakes helps keep the group warm.

◀ Sleepless in Subzero

Most birds deal with winter the same way lots of people do: They fly off to a warmer climate! Those that stick around can tough out weather as cold as -35°C, as long as they can find food. Scientists have been able to find only one kind of bird that hibernates: the poorwill. The poorwill can sleep for up to three months. During that time, its temperature drops by as much as thirty degrees. That's what we call chilling out!

Disappearing Bugs ▸

Ever wonder why you never see ladybugs during the winter? They're hibernating! Large groups of ladybugs doze together, tucked into a tree hole or other protected burrow. Houseflies and mosquitoes also hibernate during the winter months. Now if someone could only figure out a way to get those two bugs to sleep all summer, too. . . .

◂ Hot Snooze

Animals that live in warm climates often do their hibernating during the summer months. During summer dry spells, the lungfish, a fish found in African rivers, buries itself in mud and goes to sleep. It gets energy by absorbing its own muscle tissue! The lungfish sleeps until its "alarm clock"—a good rainfall—wakes it up.

"Bear-ly" Hibernating ▲

Bears are famous for taking long winter naps. But some scientists think they don't really hibernate. That's because a bear's body temperature doesn't drop much when it's sleeping. Also, bears don't sleep straight through the winter. They sometimes wake up to eat. If it's warm enough, they might even leave their dens and go exploring. Other scientists say bears do hibernate. They point out that during its winter sleep, a bear's heart rate drops to as low as eight beats per minute. That's less than half its normal rate. They also claim a bear's temperature doesn't drop while sleeping because its large body can hold a lot of heat.

Sleeping Beauties ▶

Not all butterflies hibernate. Some head for warmer winter homes. Others spend the winter as caterpillars wrapped in a cocoon. The adults that tough it out do their hibernating in caves, trees, or other shelters. How does a sleeping butterfly keep from freezing to death? As the amount of daylight gets shorter, the butterfly's blood produces chemicals called glycols. Glycols work like a car's antifreeze—they keep the butterfly's blood from freezing. Come springtime, the glycols dissolve, and the butterfly's blood returns to normal.

◀ Up to the Weather

When do frogs, lizards, and snakes hibernate? That's up to the weather to decide. Since these animals are cold-blooded, their body temperatures are controlled by the temperature of their environment. As the outside temperature drops, frogs, lizards, and snakes become more and more inactive. When their body temperatures get low enough, they begin to hibernate, often under stones or buried in mud. They keep on snoozing until warm weather wakes them up in the spring.

Katie's Letter

by Claire H. Blatchford
Illustrated by Monique Chausée

"He ate *all* my poppies," Mrs. Robinson said as she came in the back door.

"Flowers?" asked Katie, who was writing a letter to her father. "Woodchucks eat flowers?"

Katie's mother gave an unhappy nod.

Katie had only seen the woodchuck once, a dark, furry shadow rippling off across their lawn into the woods.

"He ate the peas yesterday," Mrs. Robinson added. "I don't think I can wait till Daddy returns from his business trip. I'd better call Curt."

Curt was a farmer, fisherman, and hunter with a wiry white beard and blue-black eyes. He plowed out the Robinson's driveway in the winter and helped Mr. Robinson when old trees had to be cut down. Once he'd brought a baby owl by for Katie to see before he let it go.

Curt arrived an hour later in his pickup.

"How large is this chuck?" he asked Katie and her mother.

Katie spread her arms wide.

Curt scratched his beard and grinned. "That's no baby. We'll use the big trap." He lifted a rectangular metal cage out of the back of his truck. "Got some fresh broccoli and peanut butter?"

"Peanut butter?" said Katie.

"Yup, peanut butter."

Curt spread peanut butter on the broccoli and tied it to a platter at the bottom of the cage with some string. "You want him to pull at the broccoli so the levers click and the doors shut on him," Curt explained.

"What'll we do when we catch him?" Katie asked.

"We'll take him far away. At least fifteen kilometres. Anything less and he'll be back quicker than you can hook a worm."

Katie stared at him. "How would he find his way back here?"

Curt shook his head. "Don't ask me. I just think that animals know more than we realize. A lot more. Sometimes I think they can even understand us."

The broccoli sat in the trap all afternoon, untouched. Katie watched it from her bedroom window till dark. The next morning she peered out. The trap doors were shut, but the cage was empty. Katie found the string on the edge of the lawn.

"Keep setting the trap," Curt told them over the phone. "He's bound to get careless at some point."

But the woodchuck didn't get careless. He not only cut the string and ate a lot of broccoli and peanut butter, he started on the beans, too.

Curt came by to view the damage. This time he didn't grin. "He's a smart one."

"I've seen him once," said Katie. "He hides in a hole under the stone wall when I come out."

"Will we have any garden this year?" Mrs. Robinson asked.

Curt scratched his beard. "Looks like you either put up a fence, get a dog, or shoot him."

"Shoot him?" cried Katie.

"Sometimes that's the only thing you can do. I had to shoot a chuck for the Clements last week. That critter levelled their garden two years in a row, left nothing but dirt."

"Can you put up a fence for us?" Mrs. Robinson asked.

Curt nodded.

Curt put the wire fence in deep.

For two days the garden went untouched. Then, early that Saturday morning, Katie caught a glimpse of the dark figure standing upright, sniffing the air. He was on the wrong side of the fence. He'd tunnelled deeper than Curt had dug. He'd finished the beans.

"We can't get a dog because of your allergy," Mrs. Robinson said at breakfast.

"Please, Mom, don't let Curt shoot him."

Katie's mother sighed. "I know you love animals, Katie. I do, too. But I also love my garden, and we won't have one with him around. There are woods and fields out there with plenty of food for him, but he goes right on being a pest."

"Can't you talk to him, Mom?" Katie asked. "Curt thinks animals can understand us."

"We have been talking to him. That's what we were doing when we tried the trap and the fence. We told him to stay out of our garden. He's not listening."

Katie went out and sat on the stone wall, thinking. She wished she could call the woodchuck on the telephone. She'd tell him he was smart because he got the broccoli out of the trap and he dug down under the fence, but he wasn't smart enough to stop being a pest.

The back door clicked open.

"Katie!" Mrs. Robinson called. "I'm going to the post office in half an hour. You want to finish that letter you were writing to Daddy?"

"Yes . . . I'm coming!" As Katie walked up to the house, her heart started beating hard. She stopped and clapped her hands together. Of course! She knew what she'd do—she'd write a letter to the woodchuck! She'd talk to him that way. She wouldn't mail his letter at the post office; she'd put it in the garden.

Katie found an old wooden shingle in the garage, took a red marker, and wrote on it:

Dear Woodchuck,
Please stay OUT of our garden or you will be sorry.
Love,
Katie Robinson

She climbed over the fence into the garden, pushed the shingle into the dirt, and went back to the house to finish the letter to her dad.

Curt stopped by one morning a few days later while Katie was getting ready for school.

"How are you doing with that chuck?" she heard him ask her mother.

"He's still around," Mrs. Robinson said. "I saw him yesterday near the mailbox."

"Did he try to dig his way under the fence?"

"Oh, yes, he got in once right after you put it in. Then the strangest thing happened—he lost interest in the garden. I don't know why."

Curt chuckled. "He's real smart. Some animals know when you mean business."

Katie couldn't stop grinning. She hadn't told her mother or Curt about the shingle; now she wanted to show it to them.

She ran to the garden and climbed over the fence. There were shiny green leaves everywhere. Katie lifted leaf after leaf, but she couldn't find the shingle. There wasn't a trace of it. As she knelt in the wet earth, she felt someone watching her.

Katie looked up and froze. The woodchuck was by the stone wall. He was so close, she could see his black, curved nails. They stared at each other for one long minute. Then he slid past her and headed up the drive.

ABOUT THE AUTHOR

CLAIRE H. BLATCHFORD

Claire H. Blatchford lost her hearing overnight at the age of six from mumps. That did not prevent her from going to public school or learning to read. In fact, she says that "reading became one of my favorite pastimes because you can hear perfectly when you read. You can hear into the past and into the future; you can also hear into people's secret thoughts and even into animals." This love of reading led to a love of writing, and she has had several books published.

Tree Coming Up

by Constance Levy
Illustrated by Kasia Charko

A shoot, a shoot,
A greenish boot
Kicks open the door
Of the acorn house.
A split, a crack, a baby oak
Begins to push and stretch and poke
By a worm at home in a tunnel bed,
Past ants at work,
Past beetle nooks,
Through earth as rich as brown nut-bread
Tree coming up—look out ahead!

Worms

Worms are slimy and wiggly. Sometimes they are food for animals and sometimes other animals are food for them. Their homes are underground. They like wet dirt. Usually, you can find them close to a creek.

Ants

Usually, ant colonies are big. The queen ant is the biggest ant in the colony. In an ant colony there are about eight different kinds of workers. Ants have to store food for the winter.

Mandi Steinhilber
Grade 3

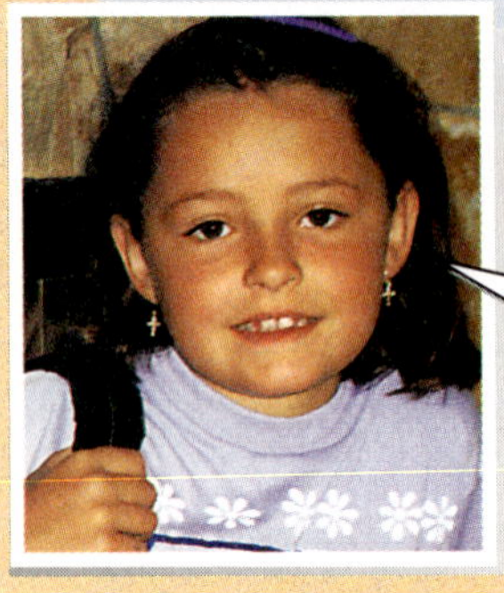

Mandi Steinhilber

Writing is fun because it helps you when you read. I think writing is hard because sometimes I don't know how to spell words. Some words don't sound out as easily as others.

A Trip in the Woods

Two weeks ago I went for a trip to the woods. I watched birds take the seeds and drop them on the ground. Then I saw a dog and cat. They had seeds stuck to them but after they rubbed against the trees the seeds fell off. I said to myself, Another plant is going to grow from those seeds. I saw some other people taking a walk and asked them if they knew how seeds grow into trees. They didn't know so I said to them, "First you need to plant the seed in soil. Then with water and sun the seed will sprout. When it sprouts the roots grow and attach to the soil under the ground. Above the ground the plant grows into a tall tree."

Nilab Osmani
Grade 3

I like writing because I can learn more words. It is a lot of fun. I like writing neatly. I got the idea for my story from a trip I went on in the woods.

Nilab Osmani

Caves and Caverns

Written and illustrated by Gail Gibbons

Deep down in the earth, people have found dark hollow places. They are called caves. Caves appear in the sides of hills or mountains, or sometimes they begin from the surface of the land and extend downward.

Some caves are small, and others are big.

Some are huge! Thousands and thousands of caves and caverns exist in many parts of the world.

Caves and caverns can be millions of years old, but they are constantly being changed and created. Sea caves are made by the pounding of ocean waves. The waves dig out the seashore cliffs, grinding away at them year after year with sand, pebbles, rocks, and boulders. This constant pounding wears the softer rock away.

Lava caves are made when lava rushes down the sides of volcanoes and hardens on the surface. Hot lava still flows underneath. When this hotter lava finally flows away, it leaves a cave behind.

There are ice caves, too. They are formed by streams that erode tunnels under mountain glaciers. The water in these streams comes from melted ice on the surface that seeps through cracks. Some ice caves begin as rock caves and then are coated with ice.

A limestone cave, also called a solution cave, is the most common type of cave. Limestone caves begin to form when rain falls to the earth, collecting carbon dioxide from the air.

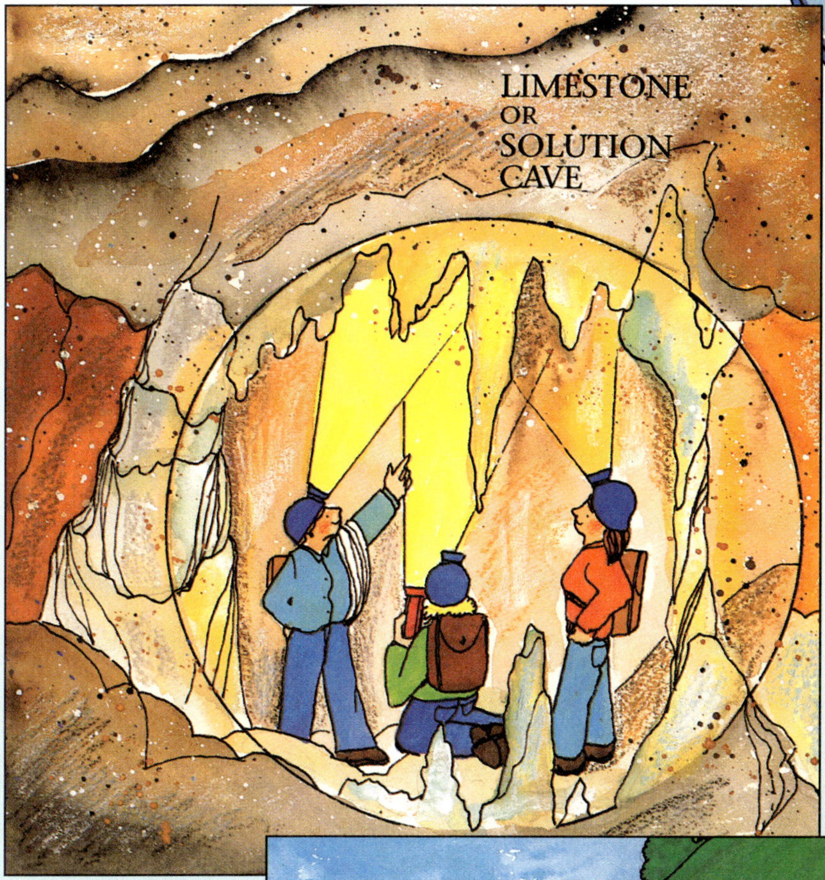

As rainwater trickles through the soil, it picks up more carbon dioxide. The water and the carbon dioxide mix together to become an acid solution called carbonic acid. As this solution seeps through the limestone, it eats away at the soft stone, making small holes.

Many years go by and the holes become bigger . . .

and bigger . . .

and bigger. The solution keeps eating away at the limestone.

Finally, when the water drains away, air enters the hollow space and begins to form a limestone cave.

The solution continues to drip into the limestone cave. Drip . . . drip . . . drip . . . It seeps through cracks in the rock.

When a drop dries on the ceiling of a cave, it leaves a tiny bit of calcite crystal. Another drop follows. It leaves behind calcite crystal, too. Drop after drop, the calcite crystals collect in the same spot. These crystals build up to form a stone icicle called a stalactite.

Drops fall to the floor of the cave, too. They build stone icicles from the ground up called stalagmites.

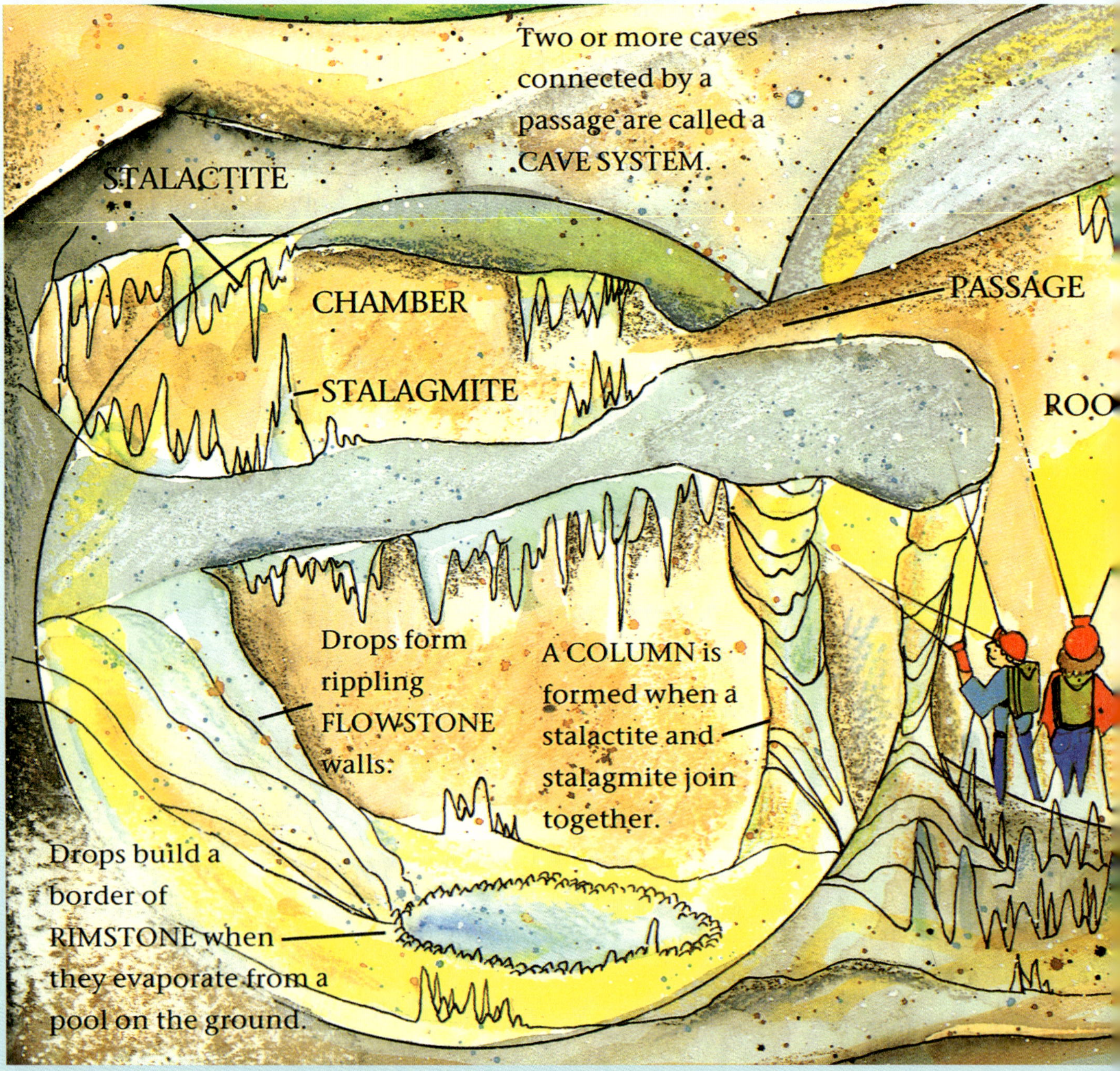

The constant dripping of the solution creates these formations, changing a cave into an amazing place of beauty. When the minerals in the solution change, layers of different colors form, too.

It takes millions of years and trillions upon trillions of drops to form a limestone cave or cavern.

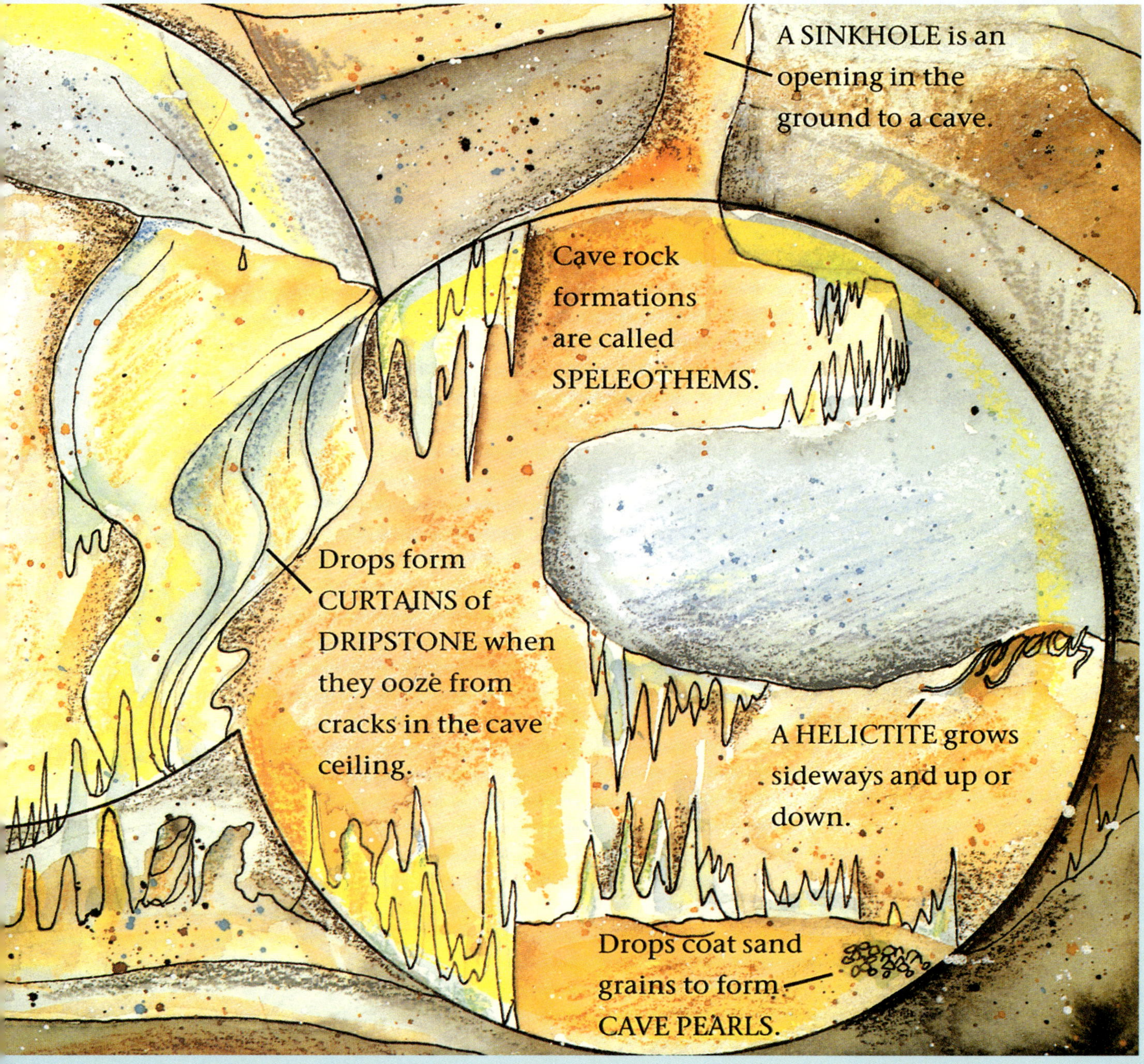

The Volcano

Written and illustrated by Ivan Gantschev

Far out to sea, a long long way from here, there is a beautiful island.

On the island there are lots of colorful trees and many kinds of animals.

There is a huge waterfall, and even a volcano that spits out fire and rocks every now and then.

Down on the beach there are turtles, and turtles, and more turtles—who look just like the stones they crawl over.

Now for as long as anyone can remember everything has been calm and peaceful on the island. But it wasn't always so. Once, long long ago, there was a great upheaval. It was all the fault of Brok, the evil giant crab who lived under the waterfall.

Brok hated everything on the island, but most of all he hated the volcano.

And so Brok persuaded the river to drill down into the volcano and put out the fire at its heart.

After many years of wearing away the rocks, the water finally reached the fiery centre of the volcano.

But the water could not put out the fire. Instead, the volcano exploded with a terrible crash.

The whole island was smashed to pieces, and even Brok was sent flying through the air.

At last, when everything had calmed down, the animals saw that the island had changed completely.

Below the waterfall, there was now a beautiful lake, where the pelicans could fish in peace.

The volcano too was quiet, and the turtles admired its reflection in the lake as they crawled slowly amongst the stones. But what had happened to Brok?

Brok the troublemaker had been thrown by the volcano onto the top of a tall tree.

A bird took the crab from the tree, thinking he'd make a good supper. But Brok smelled so horrible that the bird dropped him instead somewhere in the sea, and no one has seen him from that day to this.

And that is the story of the volcano as I heard it.

I'd like to go to that island one day and see the beautiful lake with its pelicans, and the mountain that was once a volcano. I'd try to imagine how the island used to be, with the volcano spitting out fire and rocks.

But I'd be glad enough not to meet Brok, the giant crab!

Whenever I hear of some other volcano, in another country, that has erupted, I wonder whether perhaps Brok was washed up on that shore, and has started his troublemaking all over again.

ABOUT THE AUTHOR

IVAN GANTSCHEV

Ivan Gantschev was born in Bulgaria, and he studied at the Academy of Art in Sofia, Bulgaria. Ivan's picture books have been published in fifteen languages, and his artwork has been displayed all over Europe and in Japan. He currently lives in Frankfurt, Germany.

Building Tunnels

by Etta Kaner
Illustrated by Stephen MacEachern
Photographed by Gilbert Duclos

Tunnels are usually built to make transportation easier. Many tunnels carry subways, trains, or cars. Some tunnels carry fresh water into cities and sewage away from them. Tunnels also hold gas, telephone, and electrical lines that are buried underneath streets.

Whether they are building a tunnel under city streets, through a mountain, or under water, engineers are always concerned about one thing—strength. How can a tunnel be strong enough to withstand the weight of thousands of tonnes of soil, rock, or water above it? The shape of a tunnel has a lot to do with its strength.

Which Shape Is the Strongest?

Try this experiment. You'll need:

- Plasticine or other modelling clay
- 3 strips of manila tagboard or 3-ply Bristol board, each 15 cm x 45 cm
- scissors
- some thick hardcover books

1. Make eight cubes of Plasticine, each side measuring about 2.5 cm. These are your testing weights.

2. Cut one of the strips of tagboard so that it is only about 30 cm long.

3. Use this strip to make an arch between two piles of books that are 15 cm apart. How many Plasticine cubes does the arch support?

4. Cut another strip so that it is 30 cm long. Fold the strip to form three sides of a rectangle, like this:

5. Put the rectangle between the two piles of books. How many cubes does it support?

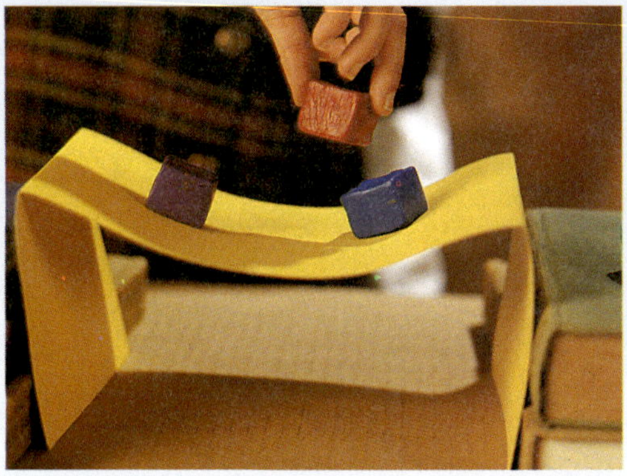

6. Use the third strip to form three sides of a square, each side measuring 15 cm.

7. Put the square between the two piles of books. How many cubes does it support?

Conclusions

The arch shape is the strongest because the weight is spread out evenly, so that no single point on the arch supports a greater part of the load. That's why the tops of tunnels are always rounded.

Many tunnels are circular. Some tunnels are horseshoe shaped, like the world's longest rail tunnel, the Seikan Tunnel in Japan. Wide tunnels that are used for two or more roads are called basket-handle tunnels. Tunnels with straight sides and a flat bottom are called vertical sidewall tunnels.

Planning and Building Tunnels

Before they plan a tunnel, engineers must know what they'll have to dig through. Soil experts drill deep into the ground and bring up samples of soil and rock. These samples help engineers decide how to build the tunnel.

Tunnels can be built through earth or through rock. The method used for digging each tunnel depends on where it is.

Amazing Ancient Tunnels

It is amazing that people in ancient times dug very long underground tunnels using only hand tools. One of the most famous was King Hezekiah's tunnel, which carried water from a spring outside the walls of Jerusalem into the city. It was built about 2700 years ago and was about as long as the CN Tower is tall. Even though the tunnel didn't follow a straight line, diggers starting at each end met in the middle. They were so proud of this feat that they recorded it on the walls of the tunnel.

Tunnelling Through Earth

If you've ever dug through earth or sand, you know how hard it is to stop the hole from caving in. Engineers have the same problem when they build a tunnel through soft earth.

The tunnel is dug with a tunnel-boring machine (TBM). This machine is shaped like a giant tin can with a huge disc or cutting head at its front. When the TBM pushes against the earth, the cutting head rotates and large teeth protruding from it dig away the earth. As the machine moves forwards, supports are put up along the sides of the tunnel to stop the earth from falling in. These supports either are concrete segments put together to make round walls or they are steel rings with wood planks between them. If steel rings are used, the tunnel is then lined with concrete.

Tunnelling Through Rock

Some tunnels are blasted through rock using dynamite. This is how the Simplon Tunnel was built through the Alps. Workers blasted through 19.8 km of Alpine mountain to build a tunnel that started in Italy and ended in Switzerland. After each dynamite explosion, the loose rock, or muck, is removed with a mucking machine. This has a giant bucket that scoops up the muck and loads it onto a train or conveyor belt that carries it out of the tunnel.

Another way to tunnel through rock is with a tunnel-boring machine, or TBM. This TBM has round steel cutters instead of teeth on the rotating disc. As the TBM pushes against the rock, the cutters cut into the rock and break it up. The rock falls through spaces between the cutters onto a conveyor belt inside the TBM. The rock is then transported to carts that carry it away.

About the Author

ETTA KANER

Etta Kaner has been an elementary school teacher for more than twenty years. She is the author of several science books for children, including *Bridges, Balloon Science*, and *Sound Science*. She currently lives in Toronto and teaches in Mississauga, Ontario.

Jonathan Cleaned Up—Then He Heard a Sound

or Blackberry Subway Jam

by Robert N. Munsch
Illustrated by Michael Martchenko

Jonathan's mother went to get a can of noodles. She said, "Jonathan, please don't make a mess!"

When she was gone, Jonathan stood in the middle of the apartment and looked at the nice clean rug and the nice clean walls and the very, very clean sofa and said, "Well, there is certainly no mess here."

Then he heard a sound. It was coming from behind the wall. He put his ear up against the wall and listened very carefully.

The noise sounded like a train. Just then the wall slid open and a subway train pulled up and stopped. Someone yelled, "LAST STOP! EVERYBODY OUT!" Then little people, big people, fat people and thin people, and all kinds of people, came out of Jonathan's wall, ran around his apartment, and went out the front door.

Jonathan stood in the middle of the living room and looked around. There was writing on the wall, gum on the rug and a man sleeping on the sofa, and all the food was gone from the refrigerator.

"Well," said Jonathan, "this certainly is a mess!" Jonathan tried to drag the man out the door, but he met his mother coming in. She saw the writing on the walls, the gum on the rug, and the empty refrigerator. She yelled, "Jonathan, what a mess!"

Jonathan said, "The wall opened up and there was a subway train. Thousands of people came running through."

But his mother said, "Oh, Jon, don't be silly. Clean it up."

She went out to get another can of noodles, and Jonathan cleaned up. When he was all done, he heard a sound. It was coming from behind the wall. He put his ear up against the wall and listened very carefully. The noise sounded like a train. Just then the wall slid

open, and there was a subway train. Someone yelled, "LAST STOP! EVERYBODY OUT!" And all kinds of people came out of Jonathan's wall, ran around his apartment, and went out the front door.

This time there were ice-cream cones and chewing gum on the rug, writing and footprints on the wall, two men sleeping on the sofa, and a policeman watching TV. Besides that, the refrigerator was gone. Jonathan got angry and yelled, "Everybody out."

Just then his mother came in. She saw ice-cream cones and chewing gum on the rug, writing and footprints on the wall, two men sleeping on the sofa, a policeman watching TV, and a big empty space where the refrigerator had been. "Jonathan," she said, "what have you done?"

Then she heard a noise. It was coming from behind the wall. She put her ear right against the wall and listened very carefully. The noise sounded like a train. Just then the wall slid open and a subway train pulled up. Someone yelled, "LAST STOP! EVERYBODY OUT!" And all kinds of people ran out of Jonathan's wall, ran around his apartment, and went out the front door.

There were ice-cream cones, chewing gum, and pretzel bags on the rug, writing and footprints and handprints on the wall, and five men sleeping on the sofa. Besides that, a policeman and a conductor were watching TV, and the fridge and stove were gone.

Jonathan went to the conductor and said, "This is not a subway station, this is my house!"

The conductor said, "If the subway stops here, then it's a subway station! You shouldn't build your house in a subway station. If you don't like it, go see City Hall."

So Jonathan went to City Hall.

When he got there, the lady at the front desk told him to see the subway boss, and the subway boss told Jonathan to go see the Mayor.

So he went and saw the Mayor. The Mayor said, "If the subway stops there, then it's a subway station! You shouldn't build your house in a subway station. Our computer says it's a subway station, and our computer is never wrong." Then he ran out for lunch.

In fact, everyone ran out for lunch, and Jonathan was all by himself at City Hall. Jonathan started to leave, but on his way out he heard a sound.

Someone was crying, "Oooooooh, I'm hungry." Jonathan listened very carefully. He walked up and down the hall and found the room it was coming

from. He went in, and there was a big, enormous, shining computer machine. The computer was going "wing, wing, kler-klung, clickety clang," and its lights were going off and on. The voice was coming from behind it.

Jonathan squeezed in back of the machine and saw a little old man at a very messy desk. The man looked at Jonathan and said, "Do you have any blackberry jam?"

"No," said Jonathan, "but I could get you some. Who are you?"

"I'm the computer," said the man.

Now, Jonathan was no dummy. He said, "Computers are machines, and you are not a machine. They go 'wing, wing, kler-klung, clickety clang.' "

The man pointed at the big computer and said, "Well, that goes 'wing, wing, kler-klung, clickety clang,' but the darn thing never did work. I do everything for the whole city."

"Oh," said Jonathan. "I will get you some blackberry jam if you'll do me a favor. A subway station is in my house at 980 Young Street. Please change it."

"Certainly," said the old man. "I remember doing that. I didn't know where to put it."

Jonathan ran out and passed all the offices with nobody there. He ran down the stairs and all the way to a jam store. He got four cases of jam. It took him three hours to carry it all the way back to City Hall. There was still nobody there. He carried the jam back behind the computer and put it on the floor.

"Now," said the old man, "where am I going to put this subway station?"

"I know," said Jonathan, and he whispered in the old man's ear. Then he left. But the old man yelled after him, "Don't tell anyone the computer is broken. The Mayor would be very upset. He paid ten million dollars for it."

When Jonathan got home, his mother was still standing on the rug because she was stuck to the gum.

Jonathan started washing the writing off the wall. He said, "There will be no more subways here."

And he was right.

ABOUT THE AUTHOR

ROBERT N. MUNSCH

Robert N. Munsch is Canada's best-selling author. He has sold over twenty million books in ten languages. Robert makes up most of his stories on the spot, and tells them over and over before he writes them down. Every year, Robert travels around North America telling stories and meeting his fans. When not travelling, he lives in Guelph, Ontario, with his wife and three children.

Caves

Caves are scary
and dark
Very dreamy
Everything is black
Scary

And gloomy
New caves
Dare to go in

Look at this bat
In the cave
Frightening
Everything is alive

David Gilmour
Grade 3

David Gilmour

I like to write about caves, and enjoy it most when I do a good job.

The reason I chose this topic is because our class was writing about something underneath the surface. Plate tectonic theory gives you information about the earth's surface and plates, and earthquakes.

Brock Hoback

The Tectonic Theory

The earth does a lot of cool things. Plate Tectonic Theory is about the shifting plates of the earth. Once the earth was all together. Then one day the earth shifted apart, causing volcanoes like Mount St. Helens. One plate goes underneath a different plate and magma comes out of a volcano. Usually people get out of the way of volcanoes. The earth also has dangerous earthquakes. Plate Tectonic Theory is one of the many mysteries of the earth.

Brock Hoback
Grade 3

The Missing Marble Case

Many years ago, in 1925, a boy stood on the porch of Gore Vale mansion (see left) with his friends. As he played with a marble in his pocket, it fell out, rolled across the porch, and over the edge into the dirt below. There it stayed until it was found by the team of dirt detectives—over seventy years later.

Meet the Dirt Detectives!

by Sheila Fairley

To find out about the mysterious case of Gore Vale mansion, which once stood in Toronto, Ontario, George and AnnMarie are searching for clues—clues buried under dirt. Along with professional diggers, they're working on a project to uncover the past. Join them as they dig back through time . . .

Sheila: How did you get interested in digging in the first place?

George: My mom told me about it and so did my uncle who's a teacher.

AnnMarie: I knew a bit about it before coming here with my class, but I had never been on a dig.

Sheila: When you first came on the dig, did you have any idea of what you expected to find?

George: I didn't really think I would find anything, but I was lucky. The first day I found a nail, some brick chips, and a piece of glass.

Sheila: Now that you've worked on this project, has it changed the way you think about the past?

AnnMarie: Before, I thought it was boring, but now I see it's not. We have two hours for a dig but it goes by so fast, it feels like a few minutes!

Tools of the Trade

The Story of Gore Vale

1820

Gore Vale mansion is built.

Sheila: What's the most interesting thing that you've found while digging?

AnnMarie: I found part of an old china dish. You could only see part of the pattern and it was very colorful.

Sheila: Was it different from the kind of dishes that we use today?

AnnMarie: Yes, the china felt like plastic.

Sheila: Is there something about digging that you don't like?

George: You have to wait for a long time and you have to go slowly. I would like to be able to go a little faster.

Sheila: If you could leave something behind for future diggers to find, what would it be?

AnnMarie: Clothes . . . baggy jeans, and polo shirts.

George: I would probably write a letter or bury a time capsule. I'd write about the things we do.

Sheila: What's the most important thing you'd like to share about digging?

George: Don't dig anywhere without checking because it may be against the law—and it could be dangerous!

AnnMarie: If you get a chance, try it—it's really fun. You have to wait, you have to be patient, and you never know when something's going to turn up. But when it does, it's a surprise.

Dinosaur Bones

Written and illustrated by Aliki

The first dinosaur I ever saw was in a book. The book said what dinosaurs ate and where they lived. It said they all died out sixty-five million years ago.

Then I went to the museum and saw dinosaur bones. I could see how big dinosaurs really were. I was glad the skeletons didn't move!

I wondered how people know so much about dinosaurs. How do they know what dinosaurs looked like if they've never seen one? How do they know dinosaurs ever existed?

For a long time, people *didn't* know. Then they began to find fossils. Fossils are the remains of animals and plants that died long ago. The animals and plants were preserved in mud or sand and slowly turned to stone.

People found fossil shells, leaves, and fish. They found fossils of creatures that no longer exist. The fossils were clues to the distant past, long before human beings appeared on earth. The more fossils people found, the more curious they became.

In 1822, in England, Mary Ann Mantell spotted some strange, giant fossil teeth in a pile of rocks near a quarry. She showed them to her husband, a doctor who collected fossils. Dr. Gideon Mantell had never seen such teeth! He searched the quarry and found a few more teeth and some bones.

Dr. Mantell said they belonged to a giant, plant-eating reptile that lived during the Mesozoic era, millions of years ago. He could tell its age from the rock the teeth and bones were buried in. He drew the animal as he thought it looked and named it *Iguanodon,* which means "iguana tooth."

Scientists laughed. A giant reptile! Millions of years old! But Dr. Mantell was convinced. He searched on, hoping to find more bones so that he would have better proof.

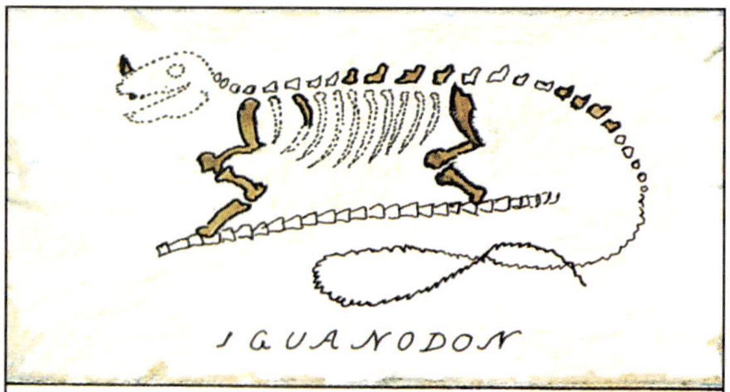

From the few bones he had found, Dr. Mantell made this sketch of an Iguanodon skeleton.

Meanwhile, people uncovered more giant fossils. Scientists studied the finds. They wrote about them and exchanged ideas and information.

Bit by bit, Dr. Mantell was proved right. All these fossils were indeed the remains of a group of giant prehistoric reptiles. Dr. Richard Owen named the group Dinosauria—"terrible lizards."

After that, there was a blaze of interest. An exhibition was held of life-sized dinosaur models. The excited public flocked to see them.

1878 More than thirty Iguanodon skeletons were found in a coal pit in Belgium. It took three years to dig them out.

People knew there must be more dinosaur bones, and there were. Fossil hunters found big ones and small ones and newly hatched babies. They dug fossils out of cliffs and quarries, coal mines and riverbanks, all over the world. Scientists pieced the bones together and gave each new dinosaur a name. Early ideas changed, and early mistakes were corrected. With every find, scientists learned more and more about dinosaurs and their world.

The earth looked different then. It wasn't separated into continents, as it is today. It was just one mass of land, surrounded by water. Dinosaurs could roam freely all over the world. There weren't many high mountains or oceans to stop them. The weather was warm everywhere—perfect for dinosaurs to thrive in. And they did thrive—for 140 million years. How do we know?

1853 The Iguanodon modeled by Waterhouse Hawkins had a horn on its nose.

After the find in Belgium in 1878, scientists knew the horn was really a thumb.

1914 A sketch of Anatosaurus by Arthur Lakes had a flexible tail.

Later, scientists discovered the tail was thick and powerful.

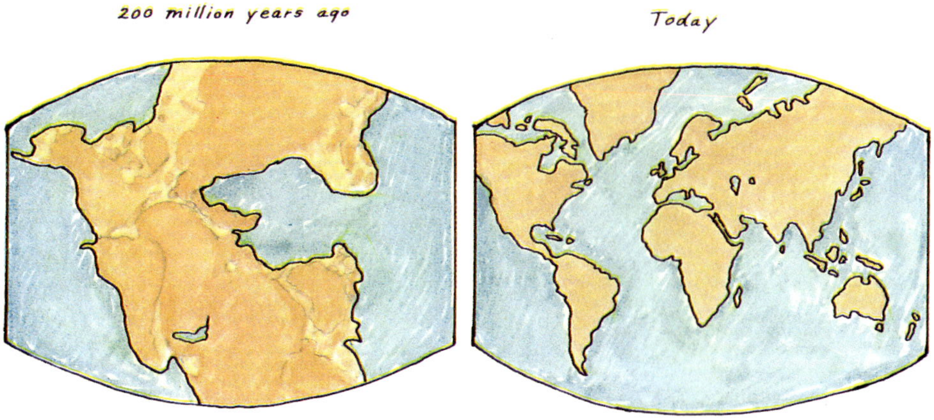

From fossils, that's how we know. Long ago a dinosaur died. Mud covered it, layer upon layer. Slowly both the dinosaur and the mud turned to stone. In time, more and more rock layers, or *strata,* built up. The rock in each layer is different, and each layer contains its own fossils. That is how scientists tell time.

Scientists divide time on earth into eras, and eras into periods. Dinosaurs lived during three periods of the Mesozoic era. We know that because their fossils were found only in those layers. In that long Mesozoic time, dinosaurs changed and developed—they evolved.

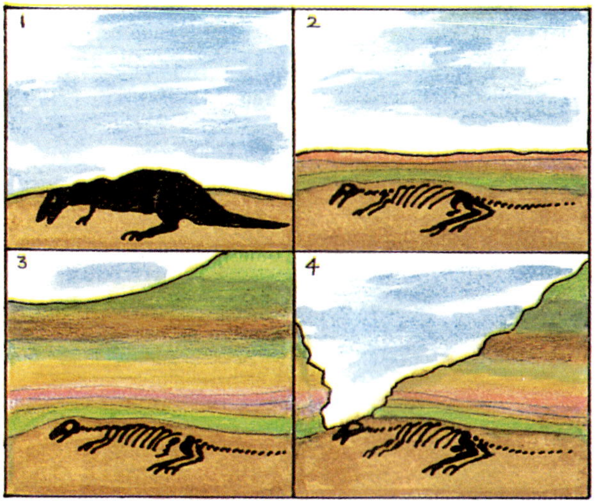

Dinosaurs first appeared late in the Triassic period. There weren't many, and they were mostly small. Then bigger dinosaurs evolved and multiplied. During the Jurassic period, many grew to huge sizes. The giant plant eaters, or herbivores, were the biggest dinosaurs ever. There were big meat eaters, or carnivores, too.

By the Cretaceous period, dinosaurs had taken over.

There were crested ones, horned ones, and armored ones. And there was the fierce king of them all, *Tyrannosaurus rex.* The dinosaurs flourished. It was their world. Then, suddenly, they all died out. No one knows why.

There are many things we don't know about dinosaurs. We wonder what colors they were, what noises they made. We wonder if they were warm-blooded or cold-blooded. Scientists search for more answers. And I check in at the museum and read my new books for the latest news.

ABOUT THE AUTHOR

ALIKI

Since her first children's book was published in 1960, Aliki has gone on to write and illustrate many award-winning books. Aliki is married and has two children. Her husband, Franz, is also a children's book writer, and Aliki has illustrated several of his books.

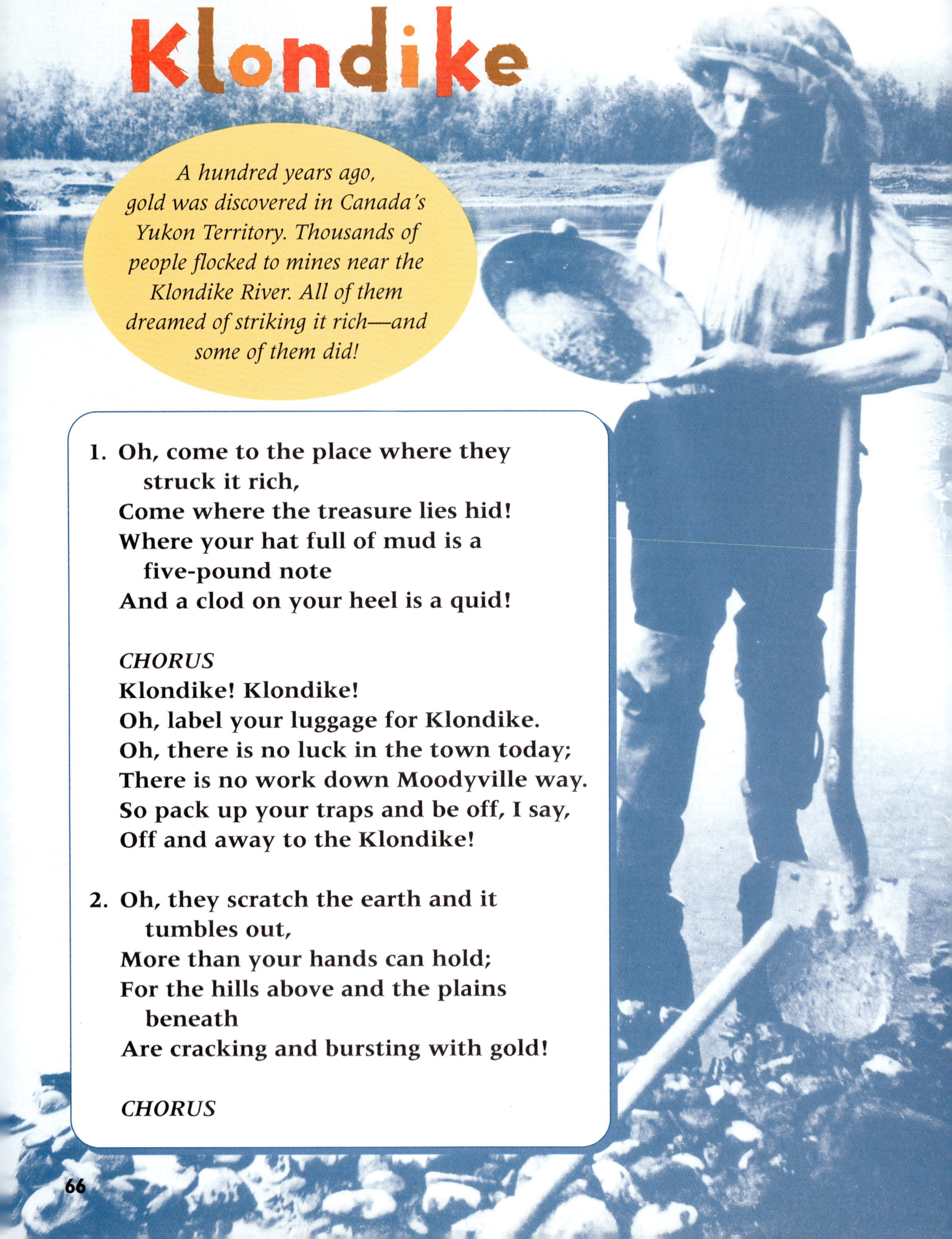

Klondike

A hundred years ago, gold was discovered in Canada's Yukon Territory. Thousands of people flocked to mines near the Klondike River. All of them dreamed of striking it rich—and some of them did!

1. Oh, come to the place where they
struck it rich,
Come where the treasure lies hid!
Where your hat full of mud is a
five-pound note
And a clod on your heel is a quid!

CHORUS
Klondike! Klondike!
Oh, label your luggage for Klondike.
Oh, there is no luck in the town today;
There is no work down Moodyville way.
So pack up your traps and be off, I say,
Off and away to the Klondike!

2. Oh, they scratch the earth and it
tumbles out,
More than your hands can hold;
For the hills above and the plains
beneath
Are cracking and bursting with gold!

CHORUS

OFFICE AT
AURORA DOCK
SECURE TICKETS BY THE
STEAMERS BONANZA KING
10 DAYS TO SEATTLE AND
COMET
ING PARLOR
P.J. Thomas Collection
C G7
1. Oh, come to the place where they struck it rich,
C
Come where the trea – sure lies hid! Where your hat full of mud is a
G7 C Chorus C F
five-pound note And a clod on your heel is a quid! Klon – dike! Klon – dike! Oh,
G7 C G7
lab–el your lug - gage for Klon – dike. Oh, there is no luck in the town to - day; There
C
is no work down Mood – y – ville way. So pack up your traps and be
G7 C
off, I say, Off and a – way to the Klon – dike!

Treasures of the Deep

by Todd Mercer
Illustrated by Malcolm Cullen

What do you imagine when you think of sunken treasures? Storms, sharks, pirates—and gold!

The Caribbean Sea is one of the best places in the world to hunt for sunken treasure. Long ago, hundreds of Spanish ships called *galleons* sailed these waters. They were carrying treasures of gold and silver to Spain. These ships faced great dangers.

Terrible storms called *hurricanes* could snap a ship's masts in two. Coral reefs could rip huge holes in boat hulls. Sometimes pirates even attacked the treasure ships. Many galleons sank with valuable treasure on board.

A Ship Sinks

One of these lost treasure ships was the *Concepción*. The galleon left Havana, Cuba, in 1641 carrying a cargo of gold and silver. On its way to Spain, the ship met a hurricane. Its masts snapped in the fierce storm, and the ship drifted for days. At last it hit a coral reef and sank. People on board threw bars of silver onto the reef to make a place to stand. To this day, the deadly reef is known as the Silver Bank.

The ship and its treasure sank to the sea bottom. The silver bars left on the reef above were soon stolen, and the site of the wreck was forgotten.

Searching for Treasure

Of course, people knew that the *Concepción* lay somewhere near the Silver Bank. Years later the wreck was found, and some of the treasure that had spilled out of it was carried away. However, the treasure in the main part of the wreck was never recovered. In 1978, the site of the wreck was rediscovered, and more treasure was found.

However, a treasure hunter named Tracy Bowden believed there was still more to be found. He and his crew started diving to the *Concepción.* They used metal detectors, earphones, and undersea lights. The metal detectors located the huge iron cannon of the galleon, which still lay on the sea floor. By this time, the wood of the ship had rotted away. All that was left was a mass of coral.

Ship's cannon covered with coral.

Silver coins and a Chinese vase from the Concepción.

Working on the wreck was dangerous. The divers had to worry about sharks, and they had to lift large pieces of coral to uncover the ship's cargo. Still, their hard work paid off. In one place, they found a damaged treasure chest. Over three thousand silver coins and a valuable Chinese vase had spilled out of it. They found gold and diamond jewellery, and other precious things, buried in the sand. A thick coral crust covered many treasure items. Only X-rays could show what was hidden inside.

What Treasures Tell Us

Treasure hunters only keep half of the treasure they find. The other half goes to the country that controls the waters where the treasure ship lies. So some of the treasures from the *Concepción* are now in museums for all people to see and enjoy. Their value is far greater than their worth in money, because they tell us much about the past. For example, the vase from the *Concepción* shows us that the Spanish once traded with Chinese merchants. Tools found in the wreck even tell us that people on board the *Concepción* liked hot chocolate!

Equipment for making hot chocolate.

More Terrific Treasures

The wrecks of other fabulous treasure ships have also been found in the Caribbean. The galleon *Tolosa* sank during a hurricane in 1724. Among its treasures were pieces of diamond-studded jewellery containing over a thousand pearls. A fleet of ten treasure ships sank off the coast of Florida in 1715. Among the treasure items found there were a gold toothpick worth more that $50 000, about a thousand gold coins, and silver coins called *pieces-of-eight*.

Treasure from the Atocha.

Mel Fisher.

However, the greatest find of all was made by an adventurer named Mel Fisher. He discovered a treasure worth more than $450 million in the wreck of the galleon *Atocha*. That's the richest treasure ever recovered from one Spanish treasure ship!

These are just a few of the great treasure galleons that sank on their way to Spain. Most of them have never been found. Who knows what riches of silver and gold still lie at the bottom of the Caribbean Sea?

A chest bulging with silver coins.

When I write a story and can't get any ideas, I think of what topic we are doing in school because I know a lot about it.

Jessica Zabinski

Rocks and Minerals

Here are some facts about some rocks that I found.

Quartz. Quartz is very hard. It is white and has shiny parts in it.

Talc. Talc is very easy to scratch. It can be scratched by a pencil lead.

Diamond. Diamond is very hard to scratch.

Do you know that some rocks are squished and cooked under the ground? I have seen bright yellow and green rocks. Some rocks have metal in them, so a magnet would stick to them. I think rocks are very interesting.

Jessica Zabinski
Grade 3

When I write, I think of three titles and then I choose the best one. I need it to be very quiet so I can concentrate. I also write my neatest.

Jennifer Kobialka

The No-Name Fossil

A long time ago in Drumheller there lived an archaeologist named Simon. He had a dog named Clueless. Clueless was a very smart dog. One day Simon took Clueless to a desert. Clueless thought, What a place! Simon began digging deep in the ground. He found a fossil and dug it up. At first Simon and Clueless didn't know what it was. They studied the fossil for weeks. Simon finally discovered it was a strange-looking dinosaur. Simon took the fossil into a museum. The people put it on display, and Simon and Clueless became famous archaeologists.

Jennifer Kobialka
Age 9